JAMIE MCKENDRICK

Drypoint

faber

First published in 2024
by Faber & Faber Ltd
The Bindery, 51 Hatton Garden
London ECIN 8HN

Typeset by Hamish Ironside
Printed in the UK by TJ Books Ltd, Padstow, Cornwall

A CIP record for this book is available from the British Library

ISBN 978-0-571-38451-8

2 4 6 8 10 9 7 5 3 1

For Xon de Ros

Acknowledgements

My thanks to the editors of the following magazines, books and anthologies where some of these poems first appeared: *Archipelago*, *Ash*, *London Review of Books*, *Oxford Review of Books*, *Oxford Poetry*, *Poetry Ireland*, *Poetry Review*, *PN Review*, *Subtropics*, *The Spectator*, *The Times Literary Supplement*, *The Yellow Nib*, *A New Divan: A Lyrical Dialogue between East & West* (Gingko), *Possibilities of Lyric: Reading Petrarch in Dialogue* (ICI Berlin), *After Dante: Poets in Purgatory* (Arc) and *The White War* by Mark Thomson (Faber).

I'm grateful to Tony Ward and Angela Jarman, who published fifteen self-illustrated poems in the chapbook *The Years* (2020), and to Graham Moss at Incline Press who published six of these poems in the letterpress pamphlet *Gifts of the Magi* (2023). My thanks also to Jane Feaver and Lavinia Greenlaw at Faber for their help and vigilance.

Contents

III. THE YEARS

I.   MYRRH

St Jerome in Self-Isolation

It may be a hideous rock I've chosen
for my stretch of picturesque seclusion
but it offers shelves and storage space galore.
What looks like a cave is actually a corridor
so I have a choice between two petrified porches,
to one of which I've rigged some primitive thatch.
I have my reading matter and a pet
to protect me from boredom and of course
my task: to render reams of holy writ.
Translating anything is bad enough
but try the Word of God, try wading through
pages of genealogy and petty-minded laws,
then heart-breaking songs out of nowhere
and sudden genius bursting forth
like a scythed chariot drawn by hippogryphs.

Horridus, atrox, the rock may be,
but tourists relish its jagged menace
and geologists pretend to explain it,
casting doubt on the timeline of creation
as set out on the first page of my opus.
The city's visible in the distance, not close
enough to infect the air but not so far
as to deter the odd pilgrim. I'm here to work
not contemplate the landscape, even if
that's what seems to excite the painters
who visit on weekends and have me pose
bespectacled in sackcloth at my threshold,
stylus in one hand, the other ruffling the beast's mane
– damn their rickety easels and their prying eyes.
And damn this Latin that's not Illyrian.

Nugget

for Michael Hofmann

The magician Márquez had a dread of gold
and wouldn't wear it. But here I am sitting through
'Aussie Gold-Diggers' – that's enjoyed a lockdown
boom, perhaps for its promise of hidden treasure, or because

these pale-skinned mates have put their lives on hold
to scour a red desert under a cruel sun
with a stick that hums then gives a wail of hope
for what – a bug-sized nugget or a rusted can?

Just yards away in the unprospected zone
– if only they'd swerved instead of keeping straight –
lies a buried glory which they'll never find.

They could almost be poets, the way they
trudge cussedly on, quite oblivious
to all the dross and mess they leave behind.

Frankincense

Flying serpents guard the incense trees
and only burning storax keeps them off.
The wounded bark exudes medicinal resin.

The third cut renders the finest grade
transported by camels then by elephants
east along the Silk Road, far as China

or west by boat to Rome and Santiago.
The serpents watch their treasure cruelly raided
for white gold squandered on cathedral aisles

in wafts of holy smoke from thuribles.
The notched bark heals by slow degrees
and a mauve silence wreathes the incense trees.

Myrrh

Consider the lilies: with the utmost care
if you're a cat, as every part
of the plant – its stem, its leaves, its pollen –
will be fatally toxic and result
in liver failure. For the rest of us,
consideration is its own reward,
a triumph of aesthetics over ethics.

They toil not neither do they spin
strikes me as the ultimate
apologia for my chosen life style
if you'd call it chosen. Or a style. I imagine
Solomon arrayed in all his glory
– cloth of gold bedecked with crimson chevrons,
wisdom seeping from his every pore.

He accepts the lily's his superior
at least in terms of temple architecture,
but then demurs, and claims the flower's merely
natural, while his songs are of a different order:
artificial, unpredictable, inwrought
with stuff he had to mine from his own heart,
blacker than rubies, fragrant as Sheba's myrrh.

Balthazar

Of black complexion and a heavy beard
according to Bede,
Balthazar has had by far
the furthest to travel, on good roads and bad.

Not a vine leaf, a palm frond, a hawk's tail feather;
not saffron, myrtle or orient sapphire –
he has meditated on the matter

following the glimmering trail of the star,
and settled on myrrh.
And not for whatever
symbolic stature it's meant to confer

– death of a king or birth of the messiah –
but for the thing itself, born of a wound,
for its goodly scent, for its resonant sound.

Smyrna

Bearing myrrh much as someone once brought crockery
to Delft, or votive candles to a shrine
already crowded with travellers' offerings,

I arrived in the port of Izmir, where Homer
was born. Either there or in Rhodes or Chios
or Salamis or Argos or Athens or Colophon or

all of them, being not one but many, being him- or her-
self a populous city and a wild frontier
and almost as old as the oldest olive trees.

Bearing myrrh and some choice scraps of history:
viz. the place was razed by earthquake in 178 AD;
in 1076 was captured by the Turks

though soon reconquered by Byzantium;
then Gustave Eiffel designed the Konak Pier
to which I moored my bark. Now, years later,

I remember only the welcome in the harbour,
the cry of the muezzin, my translator
lovely as Aphrodite, and the gift

of an inscribed quartz obelisk I eventually bore
away, though I might have preferred their
almonds and apricots, or even my own myrrh.

Myrtle

Aeneid, 3

Soon as I landed on the shores of Thrace
I slaughtered a radiant white bull
hoping the rite would please the gods of place.
Close by stood a mound covered by cornel
interlaced with a thicket of myrtle,
a tanglewood of branches every which way.

To clear that stubborn-rooted undergrowth
and deck our altar with some sprigs of green
I snapped a bough from the nearest myrtle
and what my eyes saw seized and froze
my veins with ice – the bark began to ooze
black gore, and trailed a slick of blood.

This was a mystery which I had to fathom.
I tried once more with a second branch that led
to the same result – thick gouts of blood
ominously stained my hands and sleeves dark red.

My soul quailed and I offered up a prayer
to the woodland nymphs and to Gravidus,
father deity of the Getic plain,
to stop this evil thing from spreading harm.

A third time, kneeling in the sandy soil,
I wrestled with the clustered myrtle limbs
and woody roots but then a further horror
lay in wait – a wailing tearful voice was heard,
a metal rustling sound like silver foil:

'Why, o why, Aeneas do you wound me
with yet more pain? Spare the buried dead.
Stay your pious hands from sacrilege.
I am your Trojan brother, Polydorus
slain by the king of Thrace. The blood you've shed
is actual blood, my blood, not sap. Make haste
and leave this cruel land, these murdering shores
where I fell to the spears of treachery and greed.

'Pent in a gnarled casket all these years,
a crop of jagged pikes has sprouted from
my broken ribs to form this palisade,
the wood I am, the myrtle I've become.'

Report to the Anthropological Society

The Festival of the Madonna of the Chickens was held
atop Somma Vesuvio, the semi-detached neighbour
of the Exterminator from whose crater
a few harmless ribbons of smoke, vaguely tinted
with sulphur, floated up to the heavens. Then all hell
broke loose from an orchestra of unearthly instruments,
mainly percussive and crepitant, plus a stringed contraption
and a shrill rustic oboe called a ciaramella. A few chords later
the dancing began with a dance that looked ancient Greek
– black, joyful, intricate, cathartic –
hour after hour with only a pause for lunch
on long trestles bearing provolone, prosciutto and red wine.

I expected the big chickens lugged up there in crates
to have their throats cut but they just strutted
about and squabbled, pecking up crumbs.
It was their day and they seemed to know it.
While the musicians reassumed their stations,
the god of wine festooned with a mantle of grapes
like a dolphin entangled in glaucous kelp
was nowhere to be seen but his spirit moved
among the bacchanti. Far off across the misty bay,
as the tireless capering drew to a close,
the lighthouse on the mole began to flash
its beams of darkness into the setting sun.

A Line Purloined from Paul Bowles

It was rather fun, being lost like this.
The roofs our floor, the palms our ventilators.
The stag's antlers serving as a cloudrack.

North was south, being lost like this.
It was rather fun to thread the city
with only the sodium glow to steer by.

Fun to think we would never be found.
The alleys smelled of resin and leather.
The small square with its switched-off fountain

was carding the winds from east and west.
A soiled earl lay toppled from his plinth.
It was rather grim, being lost like this

but fun as well. Correctly, we guessed
downhill should lead to the creaking docks
and docks would always overlook the sea.

Across the sea was another land.
And across that land was another sea,
though the sky was wrong for setting sail.

Still, it was fun of a sort to be lost like this.
The sardonic wildlife watching our steps.
No one to find, befriend or guide us.

No one to lend us a key or a chart
as the moon obscured itself with cloud
and the waves applauded the promenade.

The Tower of the Winds, 1974

That too solid thing, the Observatory,
quoting an Athenian prototype,
overshadowed the overgrown back garden

where I stayed all summer forty-seven
earth revolutions of the sun ago –
al-Haytham was right: eppure si muove –

and made a biro drawing of its canted square,
not quite an octagon, not quite a kite,
which I've kept and still must have somewhere.

Hardly a triumph, though not much worse
than that 1774 sketch by Jean-Baptiste Malchair:
The Observatory under Construction from the South East.

In mine, the astrological plaques are a blur,
the frieze of winds invisible. The summer passed
in warm proximity to a heavenly body.

Since then, sun and shadow have raced across the earth.
The Zodiac spins in ever faster gyres
clattering on its axis like a weathervane.

Drypoint

As the burin cuts into the copper plate
it leaves a burr behind – a jagged edge
which gathers the pitch black on its ridge
making micro-lesions on the dampened sheet.
The other end of the burin something curious
occurs – a metamorphosis: it turns into
a convex spatula to planish and erase
the marks made. The magic of undoing.
Daybreak. A clean slate. Tabula rasa.

Wrinkles are etched like stars; a line is scored
into my brow like a bone-deep wheel-rut cut
by a single thought. No burnisher exists
to smooth that out or to restore
the calm clear surface of my thoughtlessness.

Order Coleoptera, Genus *Coccinella*

The black-and-white illustrated page of ladybirds
was torn from an old entomology volume
by a vandal print dealer, and cost just a couple of quid.
Some life-sized for scale, others magnified times five,
their scarlets occult but their patterns still
bold enough to dazzle. So painstakingly attentive
was the engraver that each of these minims
perched on crumbs of soil or blades of grass – so they'd
                                        feel at home –
casts its own cross-hatched shadow, and light falls
gleamingly on the cupola of each wingcase.
If this isn't love of nature nothing is.
The handiwork of an anonymous artisan
stares down at me above my scribbler's desk
with blazing dark, with a tinge of opprobrium.

Alternative Anatomy

In the fragile hearing of the hawk moth
so much has to be suppressed
by a tamp as of felt
that cloaks the anvils on her thorax
when the world's hammer
incessantly strikes.
How else could the hinged sails
of her wings pivot so cleverly
erratic as they steer her
towards the almost blinding
source of light
and away from the horror clicks
the bats have engineered
to scan the depth of dark?

Spectral Acoustics

Hearing the noises that aren't there,
I can't hear the voices that are.

The knock of a ghostly postman
delivers a parcel of air.

Reddish

after Frost

Nothing pink can stay – not the starburst
of the fruitless ornamental cherry tree
that's no sooner here than gone;

not the blush, the 'hectic of a moment':
attraction or remorse. And nothing purple either.
Not the senatorial toga stained with blood,

nor the murex gutted to provide it;
not the primrose, though that's more durable
in flower years. Nothing violet endures – not tincture

of iodine that declines to ochre
when exposed to air; and nothing mauve: the engorged
pride and flush of pleasure is transient –

those 'mauve watermarks from beyond the grave'
Laforgue admired in Corbière's 'Rondels
pour après' perhaps excepted. Nothing scarlet's safe –

not the macaw's feathers nor the baboon's
hindparts though they get passed on. And as for
the octagons of indigo that blaze

against a beige ground – switched off in seconds
at the edge of sleep. Nothing reddish keeps
unlike the place where all its shades expire.

There nothing reigns in splendid permanence.

Less Red

The red warning is now a lilac alert,
– a blue shift, calming and cooling colour-wise –
as the black storm clouds sweep east with their
Atlantic swag. The council lorry
that dispensed the useless sandbags
has returned to claim them back. Sand
so far inland is a sorry augury
like the seagulls, ever more numerous and
oversized hereabouts, who seem to consider
our demarcations arbitrary
and land itself a transient category.

Muntjac

Sturdy, low-slung, skittish, horned, betusked,
the immigrant muntjac once more breaks into
the garden for his annual browse of weeds and whatnot.
¡Bien venido de vuelta! Welcome back! we say
in our respective tongues. Mi casa es tu casa.
The garden too – is yours as much as ours,

perhaps more yours, the way you stroll about and graze
on plants we haven't even learnt the names of
in either tongue. Our ownership's in doubt
so we're disinclined to trespass on this ground
you've reached by stealth through fields and fences,
by routes we'd never clocked, according to
a scent map that skeins and threads and loops
across the borders of our ruled enclosures.

Inheritance

I.

I cry you mercy, I took you for a joint-stool.
*   – King Lear*

The footstool my father rested his swollen feet on
I made as a boy with my own hands –
eight wood-glued mortar-and-tenon joints and two
wing-nuts so it could open flat or fold away.
A shoggly bit of carpentry, but oddly durable.
So foot-worn, the fabric had to be replaced.

Now that he lies in the earth and all his might
has vanished as if it never was, the footstool
returned to its maker, an orphaned thing.
Some piety stops me putting my feet up
on the refurbished cloth, a far lighter load but still
to have back what's been given feels all wrong,
takes from rather than adds to my inheritance,

which included his own father's ill-fitting gold ring,
that must have slipped from my finger,
so now it shines on the metacarpal of a forager
or lies in the soil or the sand somewhere
or makes crab-like forays on the sea-bed
scoured by the tides of the Tyrrhenian.

2.

In her last week lying without words
she seemed to be fretfully gesturing towards
the old oak chest-of-drawers
where, a few days after,
we found wrapped
in a flowery bath cap
the service revolver
she must have confiscated from our father.

The disposal of which
left us in the lurch:
whether, as my grandfather
in his turn had done with the gun he bought after
some credible death threats,
to toss it into the Mersey,
or to hand it in to the copshop in St Anne Street,
running for the umpteenth time a firearms amnesty.

Along with the clinker built model boat
he was wont to sail

on the placid pond of Sefton Park,
70 years post mortem,

le monocle de mon grand-père
has finally arrived

(arrived, as in reached the shore)
in sellotaped bubblewrap:

an anachronism his daughter,
my mother, must have contrived

to keep the gold frame intact,
the lens unscratched . . .

gold to ayery thinnesse beate;
crown glass ground and polished.

Spectacles I can see the point of
but an eyepiece? The lack

of symmetry, the affectation.
With a villainous scowl

I manoeuvre it over
my right eye – the blurrier one –

and lo and behold

Lunar Vista

It's sunny up there on the moon tonight –
deckchair weather, the better to survey
the chapped rims of craters, the scurvy

shapeless heaps of grey-brown dreck,
the clean sweep of a miserly horizon.
It's sunny up there on the moon no doubt.

Miles of the same unprocessed slag,
the lack of any historic monument
except perhaps one futile flag.

Call it a waste of perfectly good sunlight
but the star has fuel enough to spare
apparently, enough in its tank to keep

blazing away both night and day up there,
expending itself on thankless outer space.
This site has seen its fair share of the moon

going through her moody phases, filling up
then thinning down to a porcelain lip.
Up there the moon is basking in beneficence

while here it's cold and dark. Bright as a bean
she is, tugging at tides, and shining out
over these headstones and the yew's propped boughs.

Last Stop Before the Pier Head

I heard in my head again the old clean sound
of the bus conductor's ticket-machine
as he stood in the aisle and proudly wound
the palm-worn crank that made the lime green
spool unfurl on the 82C Dingle-bound
having stopped for the girls of La Sagesse
who climb the stairs to a raucous chorus
of 'La-La-Sausages' – provoking their glamorous sneers –
but the bus has decided to take a weird
detour past O'Connor's Bar and St Luke's
Bombed Out Church and hurtles down obscure streets
all the way to the Pier Head where it brakes
just yards away from the cast-iron bollards
and the shining waters where the ferry waits.

The Ferry

This is the ferry that goes back and forth
between the Pier Head and Birkenhead,
its funnel wide as a whale's mouth.

Wearing my oilskins and vicuña scarf
I stand at the prow like a figurehead,
caulk flaking from my forehead, clad in brine,

singing the same song over, out of tune,
as forth I fare to the coast of Malabar
then back bound south for the rocks of Cape Horn.

That was the ferry that went back and forth
where I last saw myself with dismantled head
trying in the high wind to raise the shrouds.

Far off, afloat, the merest flaunt of headland,
the blinding, heaving swell behind, ahead.

II. FAR AND NEAR

Capo chino

in memory of Michael O'Neill

. . . as from an unextinguish'd hearth . . .
    − P. B. SHELLEY

You might well have laughed to see me figure
Prometheus as poet-professor, but those last weeks
with the eagle feasting on your liver,
chained to your study-bed, hedged in by books,
− two of your own as yet unbound −
I saw the bowed head still lit with the fire you'd found.

Wake

for Michael O'Neill

Since as a kid I'd always thought of you
as iron-clad, as tough and swift as Achilles
– though to be honest, at eight, I'd never heard of him –
it hurt me even to think you had a heel
that might be wounded. Nearly sixty years on,

the invisible arrow had lodged in your throat.
The same as struck your fearless grandpa who
survived an attempt on his life in Cork
and lanced the boil of a maddened elephant
rampaging in a village near Madras.

Hard to swallow – you told me on the phone.
I shelved the fact, and didn't want to think
anything might impair your . . . what? Your light.
Your lucid voice, your laugh, your coursing insight
that always left me trying to keep up.

To José María Palacio

Antonio Machado, 'A José María Palacio'

José, my friend, has spring already
girt the birch boughs beside the river
and the bridlepaths? In the high plain of the Duero
spring hesitates, is always late, but then
arrives with breathtaking candour.
Have a few new leaves in timid yellow
unfurled on the dizzy tips of the old elms?
The acacias must still be bare
and the mountain ranges clad with snow.
Montcayo's peak, harsh white and pink,
towering in the sky of Aragon – resplendent.
Are the brambles in flower between
the grey boulders, and the daisies shining
in the fine grass? Surely the storks have
reclaimed the belltowers, pied mules must be
trudging the fields, and the farmhands
scattering late grain before the April showers.
The bees in among the thyme and rosemary.
Are the plum trees in flower? The violets
holding out? Stealthy poachers will be skulking
with partridge lures under their long cloaks . . .
José, my friend, are the nightingales
haunting the riverbanks? Go take the first lilies
and roses from the orchards one blue afternoon,
climb up the Espino, with its crown of thorns,
and lay them in a bunch upon her plot.

Autumnal

Rilke, 'Herbst'

Leaves fall. They fall from a great height
as if from the hanging gardens of heaven.
No – they seem to cry out as they fall.

And the heavy earth at night is also falling
from the clasp of stars into the lonely dark.

All of us fall. This hand is falling too.
Look at the others: it flaws all things.

And yet there's one who with gentle hands
upholds forever every thing that falls.

Skeleton Gazhal

Antonella Anedda, 'Gazhal dello scheletro'

According to one proverb the devil takes no interest in bones
perhaps because skeletons radiate such peace,

laid in display cases or in wide desert vistas.
I love their smiles composed entirely of teeth, the bald cranium,

those finely rounded sockets, the absence of a nose,
the gap around the sex and finally the hair,

that tinsel, blown away to nothing. It's not a taste
for the macabre but for the bald realism of anatomy,

for neat exactitude. To think of ourselves
shorn of skin ought to make us good-natured.

And is there a better way to enter heaven
than to return to stone, to know we have no heart?

Fallen Man

Dodging the metal barrier on the towpath
I fell from my brakeless bike and broke
my right arm and femur and lay looking
up at the cloudless clear blue January sky
as the swollen Thames sang softly by, making
bezelled eyelets on the surface, the ochre
of clay, of mud, of earth, of origin.
A kind woman locked my unscathed bike
to the railings after I'd fumbled for the key
with my good left hand in my bad coat pocket
while I awaited the ambulance for minutes, hours.
I had all the time in the world I'd fallen off
so suddenly, and with nowhere to go, of any moment,
there I lay, quite still, as time passed by.

Close Enough

for Bernard O'Donoghue

Does earth take a capital letter?
you rightly wonder.
To flatten or flatter
the planet, that seems the question.
And since the matter
concerns a translation
from Dante, a stretch of his hell where
the not-yet-dead
are already embedded
while their neighbours wear owlheads
twisted front-to-back – the horror of error –
it's hard not to hear terra and terror
as almost the same
or a close enough rhyme.

Green Angels

from Dante, Purgatory, *VIII*

Now, reader, sharpen your gaze
for here truth's covering is thin as gauze
so to pass beyond will ask for little force.

I saw that silent wan and august company
stand fixing their eyes upon the sky
poised between hope and expectancy,

and I saw two angels swooping downward –
each brandished a flaming sword,
its end blunted, instead of being pointed.

Their raiments, the green of bright new leaves,
fanned by the wind of their green wings,
rippled and fluted in folds behind their flight.

One of the pair alighted just above us,
the other opposite, so that effectively
all the souls between them were protected.

Their flaxen hair was fire that could be seen
but the eye recoiled from their countenance
confused by all that radiance . . .

[. . .]

My guide was wondering what so held my gaze
and I replied: 'Those three beacons all ablaze
that spread their fire across the southern pole.'

Then he explained, 'The four stars which shone there
this morning have now dipped below the horizon
and these three have taken up their station.'

While Virgil spoke, Sordello drew him over
and pointing where our gazes followed said:
'Look where our enemy has broken cover!'

At the open verge of the shallow valley
a serpent was sidling in, perhaps the very
one who offered the bitter fruit to Eve.

That foul stripe slid between the grass and the flowers,
occasionally raising its wedge-head to lick
its sinuous back as if to make it slick.

I didn't witness – so it's not for me to say –
how the heavenly hawks took to the air
but I saw the fell and rapid way they flew.

Hearing their green wings whir, the serpent
fled, and the angels wheeled back upwards to alight
just as they were, each on their own vantage-point.

The Memorious

Valerio Magrelli, 'Il memorioso'

Ingenious, my son shuts himself in the shower,
sticks a sheet of paper to the glass, on the outside,
and for an hour, enveloped in steam,
learns by heart the Ugolino canto.

Water and verses stream down; he murmurs on –
it costs me a fortune, but in the end
he emerges, cleansed and fragrant,
overflowing with hendecasyllables.

Threat Narrowly Averted

Your cry alerts me to the sly arrival
of the python as I sit oblivious
in our yard with my back to the threat,

and scares the snake off, much as the green angels
with swords drawn protect the shivering souls
from the evil one's nightly incursions

in that pantomime of purgatory. We could be Eve
and Adam in a different narrative
with a happy ending not requiring

any supernatural intervention.
It was likely only somebody's pet
that outgrew its vivarium, poor captive

that shed its chains and now must fend
for itself, alone and bruised, a continent
away from its own paradise, but let's pretend

it's still Eden out here, if chronically untended,
that the green conceals no camouflaged intruder,
though call no end happy till the last chord fades

and the credits roll in monumental lettering.

Petrarchan

Petrarch 164, 'Or che 'l ciel et la terra e 'l vento tace'

Now heaven and earth are hushed and the wind doesn't stir,
the beasts of the field and the fowls of the air
succumb to sleep, night's starry chariot wheels above
and the sea lies abed without the heave of a wave,

I stay awake and brood and yearn and weep:
always before me stands that sweet destructive grief.
At war within, wracked with anger and pain –
only the thought of her gives some faint relief.

So from a single clear and living fountain
flow the sweet and the bitter waters I take;
a single hand both wounds and heals me,

and since my torment is a shoreless sea
a thousand times a day I die and am reborn,
and ever further off's the cure I crave.

'We are the woeful pens . . .'

Guido Cavalcanti, 'Noi sian le triste penne isbigottite'

We are the woeful pens, the wee forlorn
paper-cutting knives and scissors
who have written in deeply dolent mood
these words which have just now reached your ears.

Now we tell you why we left our place
and stand before you, downcast, desperate:
the hand that moved us feels, it says,
haunted by things that shake the heart,

things that have so destroyed the man
and edged him so close to death's abyss
that nothing is left of him but sighs.

Now with all our might we come to plead
you treat us not with scorn but pay us heed,
sparing some pity for the one who wields us.

Neither Fish nor Fowl

Sometimes mending a poem can feel like freeing
a large fish from a caul of plastic netting,
working away with only a pocket knife
while the fish thrashes about, suspicious
that every saving cut will end its life;

but then the fish turns out to be a turtle
with gashes on its verdant mottled limbs.
You might expect a modicum of gratitude
though you'd be wrong. No sooner disentangled
the brute turns tail and heads off out to sea.

But never fear. Someone with a turtle-spear
stands ready to gaff the ingrate. Will you look, he says,
at its clumsy flippers that aren't at all
like fins or feathers. The least we can do is
put the poor thing out of its misery.

Anti-Social Media Shorts

trigger warning

Report this poem
for its lack of empathy,
its relentless gloom.

* * *

prose/poem

Call that a poem?
It's not even prose. Child of
neither rhythm nor reason.

* * *

stolen/borrowed

These fragments I have looted
from the classics
have now become a ruined jigsaw.

* * *

fan email

Finally someone other
than myself praises
my incomparable work.

* * *

vogue

Poet rocks elbow
patches and doleful loafers
shopping in Tesco.

* * *

sensible footwear

Trending poet tweets
she wears high heels to step on
old men's hands. Hats off!

* * *

step app

The 39 steps I took
before bed will swell
tomorrow's dismal tally.

* * *

innumerate

Talking of numbers,
a haiku isn't random. You can't
just add on as many syllables as you want.

Art's Travails

Michelangelo, 'I' o già fatto un gozzo in questo stento'

Hunched like this, I've got myself a goitre,
the sort foul water gives the peasants in Lombardy
or some other dismal dump, so my belly's thrust up
like a swollen mound beneath my chin.
  As my beard juts towards the heavens, the chafed nape
can feel my hump, and my breast is barrelled like a harpy's
while a dripping paintbrush decorates my face
with as many colours as a Turkish carpet.
  My loins have ascended into my belly and I use
my rump as a protruding counterweight
so it's mere guesswork where I plant my feet.
  My pelt is stretched in front while lumbar and spine,
from perpetual bending to and fro,
are arched and taut as a Syrian bow.
  In consequence whatever thoughts I have
are spavined, odd and misbegotten, for you can't
shoot straight through a barrel that's been bent.
  So now Giovanni, I beg that you'll stand up
for my abortive art, and defend my honour,
for I'm in a bad place, a worse state, and sure as winter,
I'm no painting, nor am I a painter.

Various Vices

Envy

Dead, he'd curse the other skulls
for their better teeth, as in life
the skills the skulls enclosed.

Chastity

When beauty and passion offered themselves
he found a little flaw to focus on:
a mole, a mark, a turn of phrase or maybe
a high regard for Salvador Dalí,
tolerance of Instapoetry.

Calumny

It takes harmful intent as well as malice
to construct a case and air it via
witless bullet-points on Twitter.

To find a word and make it mean
what it never meant is one device;
to damn without the faintest proof, another.

Booze

Of couse it's not the drinker's fault
– it's yours for being born, or breathing –
but when he leans in very close
with menace written on his face
it's hard to think that kinship counts.

Accedie

An iron key for which the lock is lost,
the door burnt down, the house erased,
hangs from her belt. A granite polyhedron
is all that's left to rest her head on.

Ire

The thought that someone might oppose them
is reason enough if reason were required
for rack or stake or pyre or waterboard.

Faith

Convinced the liar's lies are true
they'll march with banners to the gates of hell,
proud of what their leader's led them to.

The Wisdom Tooth

I probed its crown with the tip of my tongue
and it creaked like a bough a boy swings on.
Then with the pincer of finger and thumb
I plucked it from its loose bed like a bud
and set it on this oak table now a desk.
It was taller than I thought and like a blunted tusk,
its ivory inlaid with colonnades and courtyards,
and trees bearing the semblance of fruit –
still but ever-moving like that temple frieze
of rounded lovers wreathed around each other
in tireless ecstasy – a work of art,
thus by definition useless. And so the other,
older teeth went back to their task
of tearing the flesh of fowls and grinding wheat.

Tibet

I arrived in Lhasa by train in freezing weather.
From what I'd heard, my father would be there.
Outside the gaping entrance all was dark,
snow falling quietly like owls' feathers.

In the bustling concourse, doubling as a market,
just as I'd feared, my errant father
was nowhere to be seen.
I knew he was dead but that didn't seem

a proper excuse. I had in my pocket
a bronze coin he'd given me from the reign
of Tasciovanus, and his last letter
telling me, while in Dublin, to visit

and give his love to his old friend Joe Bewley
'who ran a marvellous place on Grafton Street
where they made jam and sold fine coffee and tea'.
BEWLEY'S ORIENTAL CAFE, he'd scrawled in capitals.

Then I saw him in his shining army cap,
sober, younger than ever, bigger and taller than me.
Resentment ebbed as I found myself wrapped
in the warmth of his bone-cricking, bearlike embrace.

Rolls Royce

Giorgio Bassani, 'Rolls Royce'

Immediately after having closed my eyes
forever here I am once more who knows how crossing
Ferrara by car
– a broad metallised saloon of foreign
make with huge
darkened windows perhaps
a Rolls –
descending once more from Este Castle by corso
Giovecca towards the pink
doodle of the Prospettiva Arch that meanwhile
slowly loomed larger within
the concave rectangle of the windscreen

The chauffeur with his high starched collar seated straight
in front of me knew very well the route to take nor did I
dream of prompting him
keen as I was to note at my left the church
of San Carlo then further on
to the right that of the Teatini
and there so early in a group on the pavement
in front of Folchini's
pastry shop
were gathered the friends of my father when he was young
most of them wearing big grey Homburgs some holding
flashy silver-handled canes
keen no desperate as I was to pass by the whole main street
of my city that unexceptional day of May or June
around the middle of the Twenties a quarter-to-
nine in the morning

Almost propelled by its own soft luxurious breath the Rolls
turned down via Madama and soon after swept
into via Cisterna del Follo
and at that point I was no more than a ten-year old
my cheeks red with the fear of arriving late for school
leaving at that very moment with my exercise books
under my arm
from the doorway marked
no. 1
there I was still rushing then turning back
towards my mother who was leaning out
from the upstairs window to check
I hadn't forgotten something
there I was just a second
before disappearing out of sight of her a mere girl
around the corner I raised my right hand
in a gesture of annoyance
and goodbye

I'd have liked to have shouted stop to the rigid
chauffeur and got out but the Rolls
bouncing softly on its springs was already
abreast of the Montagnone or rather had already passed
the walls and was speeding along wide empty streets
utterly unrecognisable to me
lined by roofless homes

Vigil

Giuseppe Ungaretti, 'Veglia'

One whole night
prostrate beside
a slaughtered
comrade his mouth
twisted and upturned
to the full moon
his swollen hands
delving into
my silence
I wrote
letters full of love

Never have I held
so hard to life

War War

Here lies
Karl Liebknecht,
who fought against the war.

At the time that he was slain
our city was still standing.
— BRECHT

This May a different Blitz.
As pictures of Mariupol's
charred blocks haunt the news
I check the internet
for the May Blitz
eighty-one years ago,
a goodly lifetime,
and find a black-and-white photo
from the *Liverpool Echo*
of a Church Street facade,
a five-storey frontage –
nothing holding it up
but spectral buttresses.
A miracle of balance.
Not a pane survives
to mark inside from out,
nothing to look in at
or out from but rubble.
The serifed capitals
on the two shopfronts
I guess were gold once:
ENGLISH & FOREIGN BOOKSELLER
with a bright advert
for fountain pens still
legible, and next door
ROBINSON & CLEAVER

Belfast Linen Manufacturers:
Grass-bleached. Hand-woven.
Gives endless wear.
A claim instantly belied.
Ashes of lye,
the sun-whitened threads
revert to grey.
Whether Roman or Gothic,
foreign or homegrown,
the books are all burnt.
In the foreground a brass
nozzled fireman's hose
lies slack as a speared snake.
That sodden, leaden light.
Not a tree, a leaf of grass,
a weed in sight.
You almost taste
burnt lath and plaster.

> *Nothing remains*
> *of these houses*
> *but the odd*
> *scrap of wall*
> — UNGARETTI

That May, my mother
told me, one of the first
incendiary bombs
dropped through their
roof in Marmion Road,
and sat fizzing in the toilet
like a giant poison turd.
Her brother Jack
who died at fifty-two
of his second heart attack,
tried to fish it out

with a fire shovel
but its fuse blew
hurling him back
headlong through the banisters.
He spent weeks with his blistered
face bandaged like a mummy
in a Sefton General ward
flirting with the nurses
(according to my mother,
not generally disposed
to be so lenient).
When the lint
was unwound,
the chemicals had sown
a crop of warts
on his smooth cheeks
which lodged for months
till they finally fell
like cankered leaves
leaving his face
rugged and pitted.
After my mother's death
I found a small photo of him
in army uniform
in her dressing-table drawer
on the back of which
she'd written 'My beloved
brother Jack, who died
5th December, 1976'
in her immaculate miniature
copybook script.
His eyes alight with wit,
you could barely see,
because of the scale,
the marks the bomb left

that May of the Blitz.

My mother lived
to have white hair.

Dandelion, so green is the Ukraine.
                   – CELAN

Under artillery fire
courage is expendable:
it grinds the nerves down,
a soldier once told me.
Tainted by looking,
by looking on,
it's hard to tell
through the screens
of our devices
how much worse
is worse, how near is far,
how far is near.

III.   THE YEARS

Ah, no, the years, O!
– THOMAS HARDY, 'During Wind and Rain'

Quand'io mi volgo indietro a mirar gli anni
           – PETRARCH CCXCVIII

Nothing Doing

I stopped today to watch a heron hunched
on a float beside the local swimming pool
– left undrained to shiver through the winter –
surveying the clear water with a gaze
of sheer disgust. What sort of water's
this where nothing moves that's worth a sprat?
Water that looks like water but
isn't. So poor it might as well be air.

I know the feeling. I feel the knowledge
of that heron. The world is a con.
My quiff quivers. My shoulders hunch. My beak
is sharp as a tack, as a hatchet's edge
but nothing swims or glints or gazes back
beneath the surface of the pond I scan.

Doing Nothing

A life of doing nothing is a life
well-lived, is casting shadow only where
other shadows live, doing no other life
real harm, like eating only roadkill.
Granted, it's not as if it does much good,
or makes the dark light, but at least it leaves
the dark intact, or even audible,
as inky grains sift through the atmosphere

slowing their cadence to a serenade.
So when I'm doing nothing, let's be clear,
I'm listening out across unmeasured space
for the pulse of yesteryear or – who can say –
the yet-unfurled. Call it a waste of space
but a waste seeded with luxuriant weeds.

The Thurn-Harrier

The thurn was harried from his home
by a bailiff beetle with an acid aura
in a waistcoat grand and red as Rome.

By then the thurn was utterly alone.
Rain turned to ice on his ruffled brow.
The thurn was harried from his home.

He stuffed some pamphlets in his case,
half a loaf and a chunk of lava.
The sun was dull as tarnished chrome.

The thurn's vocabulary was sparse
but still had room for several curses
he said to himself as he fled his home.

The harrier thus had earned his hire.
The thurn was harried from his home.

The Lion-Tree

Alexander Cornelius mentions a tree called the lion-tree, the timber of which he says was used to build the Argo . . . which cannot be rotted by water or destroyed by fire . . . This tree is, so far as I am aware, unknown to anyone else.

— PLINY THE ELDER

It may well be extinct, and our one authority

is terse, but that surely speaks in his favour.
No wonder its timber was used on the Argo
– the ship that rent old Neptune's slumber –
for in contact with seawater it neither rotted

nor buckled. A solitary, an isolate, it never
grew in groves but thrived in the vicinity
of clear springs. Spindly, tougher
than oak, more close-grained than gopherwood,

even its leaves, which were glaucous and spiky,
were defended against all folivores
except giraffes. Its small hard fruits, swathed
in bluish wool, were inedible and bitter

though only mildly toxic. It bore not the least resemblance
to a lion unless the noise the wind made
rattling its leaves gave rise to the name.
Perhaps it was the furious winds that finished it or else

the tree at last grew tired of existence.

Court of the Lions

Who can tell, with hard and soft so close,
liquid from solid, marble from water? Which flows?
– IBN ZAMRAK

After fifty years to revisit the Alhambra and witness
the same water spewing from the lion's maw:
I remember wearing a silver short-sleeved shirt
adorned with dragons, and for the first time,

on the airport runway, hearing the night alive
with the cicadas' tiny anvils. This time, the metal plate
screwed to my femur vibrates to their call, my heart
to the murmur of marble, the patter of water.

Mersey Foghorns

On the stroke of twelve every New Year's Eve
the boats assembled in the estuary
let loose their growling hoot, the long drawn note
on Neptune's harsh bassoon, into the dark

between us and the far shore of Port Sunlight,
cramming the black vault of heaven
with the Mersey's immemorial miseries,
in one sweary jubilant answering-back.

Dark River

There's still some ink left in the inkwell
– the last of it – to seed the storm clouds
cloaking the uplands, and just enough to fill

the river with shadow layered on shadow.
Are those flecks that float grey gulls or geese?
The rows beyond are they graves or vineyards,

alleys of hornbeam or derelict mills?
Trapped in the dark shaft, the fledgling jackdaw
finally climbs out of the fireplace in a caul

of cobwebs, flashing its azure eyes,
and now must summon all
of its fight to stay here where there's still

some grains of light, some air somehow.

Afterquake

By some cosmic quirk the disconnected phone
unleashed a scarlet squeal. – I pounced.
Before the apology expired I asked and got
the wrong number the voice had tried,

so for a whole year without a single bill
I owned those magic digits to dispense
– only for incoming not outgoing calls
but a tiny lifeline to the ancient flat

in via Torquato Tasso I shared with the din
of Cerberus barking in the courtyard – forget the rat –
and a crack the earthquake left in the vaulted ceiling.

Thirty years on, in the small dark hours,
I reach for the black Bakelite receiver
to hear the music of Venus receding.

Viaduct

Homage to André Kertész

Glad Nero's still playing Bach on his violin
you said with your usual historical acumen
in the ongoing months of the pathogen.
So here I am, weighed down with years and this
portfolio of architectural follies
which I'm toting through the bombed acres ochre
with brickdust and strewn with charred shutters.

Now bulk-buyers have emptied the pharmacy
and the bakery's boarded up, it's miraculous
the overarching viaduct is still intact –
though who travels where and why, I wonder.
I'm headed for the café where you wait
wearing your stagey satin widow's weeds
and lunar pallor in the corner seat,

a mordant update on the hallowed muse.
Disaster invests the smallest bug
with meaning, and favours superstition.
Mine's the vain thought that only you
could understand the images or else
only if you understood them could they
issue forth to cast an earthly shadow,

the scattered city rising from its ruins.

Labyrinth

See how the obstacles proliferate.

The street is gridlocked so I leave the car
and go on foot. Asking the way
I'm shown a map too miniature to read:
each road a cul-de-sac, a capillary tourniquet'd.
To reach my destination I must climb
a street so steep its aspect is a wall.
Just ten steps on, I'm breathing heavily.
The clouds above like meagre, whitened lungs.

Two women, laughing, lead me through a house
they say's a shortcut but it seems a labyrinth
of clothes-racks, curtains, shrouded furniture.
Whole families camped in halls, on balconies.
They warn me that a bull waits in the courtyard
I have to cross to reach the padlocked gate,
but instead of the bull I find a bear
that rears up, its teeth and claws unsheathed.

I carefully stroke its shoulder muttering
soft endearments to calm its maddened roars.
How low its forehead is, how sad its eyes.
If I should stop the lulling syllables
how soon before the fit of rage returns?
And by now I'm late, perhaps too late to meet
the person, waiting close by, who had promised
to liberate me from these obstacles.

An Infestation of Ladybirds

Every year now, in early October,
at the misty hem of warm and cold,
begins the infestation of ladybirds,

first one, then ten, then several hundred,
a red, black-speckled multitude.
They occupy the cramped space of the bathroom

window frame, which still bears the molecules of scent
from their previous visitation. This means
not opening the window for months until

their clamorous awakening in the spring.
For now they sleep, suspended, dreamless,
like a crew venturing into deep space.

To rouse them prematurely would be fatal.

The Register

I can still see them all, as if they'd just
gathered in red and grey for morning roll call
and fifty-five long years had never passed.

Walwyn who says little and spends his spare time
winding wire round gaudy plumes to hook
imaginary fish. Barnes from Tripoli plagued by

asthma – who has a seraphic singing voice.
Rana, the athlete from Nepal, now stocky but
somehow the same, exporting cigarettes

and tyres to China. Timmi, a gentle Yoruba,
the tallest boy by far, who died of AIDS
seven years ago, a famous photographer.

Griffin, hard to look at he was so
unbearably beautiful, who once stopped me on the stairs
and decided 'You don't like me, do you?'

I hadn't the heart to say it wasn't so.
I can still see their names engraved in the register:
Lashkari, Maw, Sajadhi, Sewell, Singh –

the hockey captain who was spared the barber.
We all began in gladness regardless of
the louring prisonhouse we'd been confined in.

He Be Me

When I arranged a meeting with my self
predictably *he* – as I'll call him – turned up late.

I had perched an hour on the barstool and drained
three glasses of red when he wafted in,

looking like me only longer-haired, years younger,
with an insouciant air and the feeblest excuse.

The barmaid I'd flirted with to no avail
as the clock dust gathered was suddenly all smiles.

I offered him a drink as it was clear
he had no money, no job, no staying power

– none of which I myself had that much of
but at least I'd arrived on time, time being

what I had less of, which made his lateness
even worse. I could tell he didn't know

what he wanted – to drink, to have, to be.
A vaguely startled look patrolled his eyes

as if his confidence was just a bluff.
I could have told him that what lay ahead

would test a sturdier confidence than his
but why waste words – he'd find out soon enough.

All the fool seemed utterly sure of
was never in his life would he be me.

Twin Peaks

the volcano
I'd christened Mont D'Espoir *or* Mount Despair
– ELIZABETH BISHOP, 'Crusoe in England'

The twin peaks of Mont D'Espoir and Mount Despair
keep changing places and are hard to tell
apart – their simple binaries of sol y sombra.

Relentless weather treats them both the same
– clouds gather at their summits and disperse.
Sometimes the clouds speak dragonish, and sometimes human.

The twin peaks are made of the selfsame stuff –
a composite of jet and alabaster,
ground down at the same rate by the same blasts.

I built a cabin at the foot of one
though now I'm not sure which of them it was.
Their spires and spurs and spars have merged.

First one seems higher, then the other
but never the one appears without its twin.
Both command the same cheerful, desperate vista.

L'amor che move il sole e l'altre stelle

I came to tend – I lie – to *visit* the grave of a friend
and found an ugly shrub with waxy leaves
had made the plot its home. Since my last attendance

ten years had passed – doing I can't think what,
except translate a dead man's words – and now
the whole granite headstone was obscured

by brambles and weeds and this excrescence.
All overgrown. My friend had somehow ended up
in a thicket of Cyrillic, the White Russian sector

who have cared a lot better for their lost ones.
Or so you'd think if love were judged like that.
Now that I'm older than he ever was,

in far worse nick than he would have been,
I dimly sense how we're the wrong way round.
Him under, me standing on the ground.

I snapped some branches from the shrub
half-expecting a hurt, indignant voice
to bubble up – bobok! bobok! – from the ragged

limbs – a reproach for the failure of
our friendship, the careless words, the disregard,
after the heaven-haven of the early years.

Now at least his name can be read, though not
the words we had the mason carve below,
the untranslated last line of *Paradiso*.

Notes

The first line in 'A Line Purloined . . .' is purloined from Paul Bowles's *Let it Come Down*.

In 'Reddish' the reference is to Robert Frost's 'Nothing Gold Can Stay' and the phrase 'a hectic of a moment', describing a blush, is taken from John Florio's translation of Michel Montaigne.

In 'War War', the margin quotes from Bertolt Brecht, Giuseppe Ungaretti and Paul Celan are my own translations.

In 'The Thurn-Harrier', the thurn is a small leaf-chewing, tree-hopping insect, as yet unknown to entomologists, but a close relative of the thorn bug.

The epigraph for 'The Lion-Tree' is taken from H. Rackham's translation of Pliny the Elder.

The epigraph for 'Court of the Lions' is my own version of lines from Ibn Zamrak's poem carved around the Alhambra fountain's basin.

The title of 'L'amor che move il sole e l'altre stelle' is the last line of Dante's *Commedia* and 'Bobok' is the title of a Fyodor Dostoyevsky short story set in a graveyard. In Russian it means 'little bean' but in the story it's a macabre and senseless sound.